50 Souls of Southern Cooking Recipes

By: Kelly Johnson

Table of Contents

- Fried Chicken
- Shrimp and Grits
- Chicken and Waffles
- Biscuits and Gravy
- Jambalaya
- Gumbo
- Cornbread
- Hoppin' John
- Collard Greens
- Pulled Pork BBQ
- Pecan Pie
- Catfish Po' Boy
- Crawfish Etouffee
- Red Beans and Rice
- Fried Green Tomatoes
- Southern Biscuits
- Banana Pudding

- Sweet Potato Pie
- Black-eyed Peas
- Chicken Fried Steak
- Pralines
- Brunswick Stew
- Pimento Cheese
- Po' Boy Sandwiches
- Low Country Boil
- Oysters Rockefeller
- Baked Macaroni and Cheese
- Fried Okra
- Chicken and Dumplings
- Sausage Gravy
- Shrimp Creole
- Peach Cobbler
- Beignets
- Bourbon Street Steak
- Muffuletta Sandwich
- Southern-style Deviled Eggs

- Southern Corn Pudding
- Collard Greens and Ham Hocks
- Pecan-Crusted Chicken
- Chicken and Sausage Gumbo
- Country Ham
- Boiled Peanuts
- Sweet Tea
- Fish Fry
- Chitlins (Chitterlings)
- Grits Casserole
- Fried Catfish
- Chicken-Liver Pâté
- Baked Beans with Bacon
- Mississippi Mud Pie

Fried Chicken

Ingredients:

- 4 chicken thighs (bone-in, skin-on)
- 2 cups buttermilk
- 1 tbsp hot sauce
- 2 cups all-purpose flour
- 1 tbsp garlic powder
- 1 tbsp onion powder
- 1 tbsp paprika
- Salt and pepper to taste
- Vegetable oil for frying

Instructions:

1. Mix buttermilk and hot sauce in a bowl. Soak chicken in the mixture for at least 2 hours.
2. In a separate bowl, combine flour, garlic powder, onion powder, paprika, salt, and pepper.
3. Heat oil in a frying pan over medium-high heat.
4. Dredge chicken in the flour mixture, shaking off excess.
5. Fry chicken for 10-12 minutes on each side, or until golden brown and cooked through.
6. Drain on paper towels and serve hot.

Shrimp and Grits

Ingredients:

- 1 lb shrimp, peeled and deveined
- 1 tbsp olive oil
- 1 tbsp butter
- 2 cloves garlic, minced
- 1 cup grits
- 4 cups water or chicken broth
- 1/2 cup heavy cream
- 1/4 cup Parmesan cheese, grated
- 1 tbsp lemon juice
- Salt and pepper to taste
- Fresh parsley for garnish

Instructions:

1. In a saucepan, bring water or chicken broth to a boil. Add grits and reduce heat. Stir occasionally for 20-25 minutes until thickened.

2. Stir in cream and Parmesan cheese. Season with salt and pepper, then keep warm.

3. Heat olive oil and butter in a skillet. Add garlic and shrimp, cooking for 2-3 minutes per side until pink and cooked through.

4. Stir in lemon juice, season with salt and pepper, and serve shrimp over the grits. Garnish with fresh parsley.

Chicken and Waffles

Ingredients:

- 2 chicken breasts (boneless and skinless)
- 1 cup buttermilk
- 1 cup flour
- 1 tsp paprika
- 1 tsp garlic powder
- 1/2 tsp cayenne pepper
- Salt and pepper to taste
- Vegetable oil for frying
- 4 waffles (store-bought or homemade)
- Maple syrup for serving

Instructions:

1. Soak chicken breasts in buttermilk for at least 1 hour.
2. In a bowl, mix flour, paprika, garlic powder, cayenne, salt, and pepper.
3. Heat oil in a pan over medium-high heat. Coat chicken in the flour mixture and fry for 6-8 minutes on each side, until golden and cooked through.
4. Serve chicken over warm waffles, drizzling with maple syrup.

Biscuits and Gravy

Ingredients:

- 1 package refrigerated biscuits
- 1 lb breakfast sausage
- 1/4 cup flour
- 2 cups milk
- Salt and pepper to taste

Instructions:

1. Bake biscuits according to package instructions.
2. In a skillet, cook sausage over medium heat until browned and crumbled.
3. Sprinkle flour over sausage and cook for 1-2 minutes.
4. Gradually whisk in milk and cook until the gravy thickens. Season with salt and pepper.
5. Serve gravy over warm biscuits.

Jambalaya

Ingredients:

- 1 lb chicken thighs, cubed
- 1/2 lb andouille sausage, sliced
- 1 bell pepper, diced
- 1 onion, diced
- 2 celery stalks, diced
- 3 cloves garlic, minced
- 1 1/2 cups long-grain rice
- 1 can diced tomatoes (14.5 oz)
- 2 1/2 cups chicken broth
- 1 tbsp Cajun seasoning
- 1/2 tsp thyme
- 1/2 lb shrimp, peeled and deveined
- Salt and pepper to taste

Instructions:

1. In a large pot, brown chicken and sausage. Remove and set aside.
2. In the same pot, sauté bell pepper, onion, celery, and garlic for 5 minutes.
3. Add rice, tomatoes, chicken broth, Cajun seasoning, thyme, and bring to a boil.

4. Reduce heat, cover, and simmer for 20 minutes.

5. Add shrimp, cover, and cook for an additional 5-7 minutes, until shrimp are pink.

6. Season with salt and pepper and serve.

Gumbo

Ingredients:

- 1 lb chicken thighs, chopped
- 1/2 lb sausage, sliced
- 1 onion, diced
- 1 bell pepper, diced
- 2 celery stalks, diced
- 3 cloves garlic, minced
- 1/4 cup flour
- 4 cups chicken broth
- 1 can diced tomatoes (14.5 oz)
- 1 bay leaf
- 1 tsp thyme
- 1 tsp paprika
- 1/2 tsp cayenne pepper
- 1/2 lb shrimp, peeled and deveined
- Cooked rice for serving

Instructions:

1. Brown chicken and sausage in a large pot. Remove and set aside.

2. In the same pot, cook onion, bell pepper, celery, and garlic for 5 minutes.

3. Stir in flour and cook for 2 minutes.

4. Add chicken broth, tomatoes, bay leaf, thyme, paprika, and cayenne. Bring to a boil.

5. Reduce heat, return chicken and sausage to the pot, and simmer for 30 minutes.

6. Add shrimp and cook for another 5 minutes.

7. Serve over cooked rice.

Cornbread

Ingredients:

- 1 cup cornmeal
- 1 cup all-purpose flour
- 1/4 cup sugar
- 1 tbsp baking powder
- 1/2 tsp salt
- 1 cup milk
- 1/2 cup butter, melted
- 2 eggs

Instructions:

1. Preheat oven to 400°F (200°C).
2. Grease a baking pan.
3. In a bowl, mix cornmeal, flour, sugar, baking powder, and salt.
4. Add milk, butter, and eggs, stirring until smooth.
5. Pour batter into the pan and bake for 20-25 minutes, until golden brown.

Hoppin' John

Ingredients:

- 1 lb black-eyed peas, soaked overnight
- 1 smoked ham hock
- 1 onion, diced
- 1 bell pepper, diced
- 2 cloves garlic, minced
- 1 1/2 cups long-grain rice
- 3 cups chicken broth
- 1 tsp thyme
- Salt and pepper to taste

Instructions:

1. In a large pot, combine peas, ham hock, onion, bell pepper, garlic, chicken broth, and thyme. Bring to a boil.
2. Reduce heat and simmer for 45 minutes.
3. Add rice, cover, and cook for an additional 20-25 minutes, until rice is tender.
4. Season with salt and pepper and serve.

Collard Greens

Ingredients:

- 1 bunch collard greens, chopped
- 1 onion, diced
- 2 cloves garlic, minced
- 2 cups chicken broth
- 1 tbsp vinegar
- 1 tsp sugar
- Salt and pepper to taste

Instructions:

1. In a large pot, sauté onion and garlic until soft.
2. Add collard greens, chicken broth, vinegar, and sugar.
3. Bring to a boil, then reduce heat and simmer for 45 minutes, until tender.
4. Season with salt and pepper and serve.

Pulled Pork BBQ

Ingredients:

- 4 lb pork shoulder
- 1/4 cup brown sugar
- 2 tbsp paprika
- 1 tbsp garlic powder
- 1 tbsp onion powder
- 1 tsp cumin
- 1 tsp cayenne pepper
- 1 1/2 cups BBQ sauce
- Buns for serving

Instructions:

1. Preheat oven to 300°F (150°C).
2. Rub pork shoulder with brown sugar, paprika, garlic powder, onion powder, cumin, and cayenne.
3. Place pork in a roasting pan and cover with foil. Roast for 4-5 hours, until tender.
4. Shred the pork using forks and mix with BBQ sauce.
5. Serve on buns.

Pecan Pie

Ingredients:

- 1 1/2 cups pecan halves
- 1 cup corn syrup
- 1 cup brown sugar
- 4 large eggs
- 1/4 cup melted butter
- 1 tsp vanilla extract
- 1/4 tsp salt
- 1 pie crust

Instructions:

1. Preheat oven to 350°F (175°C).
2. Whisk together corn syrup, brown sugar, eggs, butter, vanilla, and salt.
3. Stir in pecans and pour into the pie crust.
4. Bake for 50-60 minutes, until set.
5. Let cool before serving.

Catfish Po' Boy

Ingredients:

- 4 catfish fillets
- 1 cup cornmeal
- 1/2 cup flour
- 1 tsp paprika
- 1/2 tsp cayenne pepper
- Salt and pepper to taste
- 2 cups vegetable oil for frying
- 4 hoagie rolls
- Lettuce, tomatoes, pickles for garnish
- Remoulade sauce or tartar sauce

Instructions:

1. In a bowl, mix cornmeal, flour, paprika, cayenne, salt, and pepper.
2. Dredge catfish fillets in the cornmeal mixture, coating evenly.
3. Heat oil in a skillet over medium heat. Fry fillets for 3-4 minutes on each side until golden and crispy.
4. Toast hoagie rolls and spread with remoulade or tartar sauce.
5. Assemble the po' boys with fried catfish, lettuce, tomato, and pickles. Serve hot.

Crawfish Etouffee

Ingredients:

- 1 lb crawfish tails
- 1/4 cup butter
- 1/4 cup flour
- 1 onion, diced
- 1 bell pepper, diced
- 2 celery stalks, diced
- 3 cloves garlic, minced
- 2 cups chicken broth
- 1 can diced tomatoes (14.5 oz)
- 1 tsp paprika
- 1 tsp thyme
- Salt and pepper to taste
- 1 tbsp parsley, chopped
- Cooked rice for serving

Instructions:

1. In a large skillet, melt butter over medium heat. Stir in flour and cook for 2 minutes to create a roux.
2. Add onion, bell pepper, celery, and garlic, and cook for 5 minutes.

3. Stir in chicken broth, tomatoes, paprika, thyme, salt, and pepper. Bring to a simmer for 10 minutes.

4. Add crawfish tails and cook for another 5-7 minutes.

5. Serve over cooked rice and garnish with parsley.

Red Beans and Rice

Ingredients:

- 1 lb red kidney beans, soaked overnight
- 1 smoked sausage, sliced
- 1 onion, diced
- 1 bell pepper, diced
- 2 celery stalks, diced
- 3 cloves garlic, minced
- 4 cups chicken broth
- 1 tsp thyme
- 1 tsp paprika
- 1/2 tsp cayenne pepper
- Salt and pepper to taste
- Cooked rice for serving

Instructions:

1. In a large pot, sauté sausage, onion, bell pepper, celery, and garlic until softened.
2. Add beans, chicken broth, thyme, paprika, cayenne, salt, and pepper.
3. Bring to a boil, reduce heat, and simmer for 1 1/2 hours, or until beans are tender.
4. Serve over cooked rice.

Fried Green Tomatoes

Ingredients:

- 4 green tomatoes, sliced
- 1 cup cornmeal
- 1/2 cup flour
- 1 tsp garlic powder
- Salt and pepper to taste
- 1/2 cup buttermilk
- 1/2 cup vegetable oil for frying

Instructions:

1. In a shallow bowl, mix cornmeal, flour, garlic powder, salt, and pepper.
2. Dip tomato slices in buttermilk, then dredge in the cornmeal mixture.
3. Heat oil in a skillet over medium-high heat. Fry tomatoes for 3-4 minutes on each side until golden.
4. Drain on paper towels and serve hot.

Southern Biscuits

Ingredients:

- 2 cups all-purpose flour
- 1 tbsp baking powder
- 1/2 tsp salt
- 1/2 cup cold butter, cubed
- 3/4 cup buttermilk

Instructions:

1. Preheat oven to 450°F (230°C).
2. In a bowl, mix flour, baking powder, and salt. Cut in butter until the mixture resembles coarse crumbs.
3. Add buttermilk and stir until just combined.
4. Turn dough onto a floured surface and gently knead. Roll out to 1-inch thickness and cut into circles.
5. Place biscuits on a baking sheet and bake for 12-15 minutes, until golden brown.

Banana Pudding

Ingredients:

- 3 cups whole milk
- 1/2 cup sugar
- 3 large eggs
- 1/4 cup cornstarch
- 1/2 tsp vanilla extract
- 1 box vanilla wafers
- 3 ripe bananas, sliced

Instructions:

1. In a saucepan, whisk together milk, sugar, eggs, and cornstarch. Cook over medium heat, stirring constantly, until thickened (about 5-7 minutes).
2. Remove from heat and stir in vanilla extract.
3. In a serving dish, layer vanilla wafers, banana slices, and pudding. Repeat layers.
4. Refrigerate for at least 2 hours before serving.

Sweet Potato Pie

Ingredients:

- 2 medium sweet potatoes, boiled and mashed
- 1/2 cup sugar
- 1/2 cup brown sugar
- 1 tsp cinnamon
- 1/2 tsp nutmeg
- 1/4 tsp salt
- 2 eggs
- 1/2 cup evaporated milk
- 1 tbsp butter, melted
- 1 tsp vanilla extract
- 1 pie crust (store-bought or homemade)

Instructions:

1. Preheat oven to 350°F (175°C).
2. In a bowl, combine mashed sweet potatoes, sugar, brown sugar, cinnamon, nutmeg, and salt.
3. Beat in eggs, evaporated milk, butter, and vanilla until smooth.
4. Pour mixture into pie crust and bake for 45-50 minutes, until set.
5. Let cool before serving.

Black-eyed Peas

Ingredients:

- 1 lb black-eyed peas, soaked overnight
- 1 smoked ham hock
- 1 onion, diced
- 2 cloves garlic, minced
- 1 bell pepper, diced
- 4 cups chicken broth
- 1 tsp thyme
- Salt and pepper to taste

Instructions:

1. In a large pot, combine peas, ham hock, onion, garlic, bell pepper, and chicken broth.
2. Bring to a boil, reduce heat, and simmer for 45 minutes, until peas are tender.
3. Season with thyme, salt, and pepper and serve.

Chicken Fried Steak

Ingredients:

- 4 beef steaks (cube steaks)
- 1 cup flour
- 1 tbsp garlic powder
- 1 tbsp onion powder
- Salt and pepper to taste
- 1 egg, beaten
- 1 cup buttermilk
- Vegetable oil for frying

Instructions:

1. In a shallow bowl, mix flour, garlic powder, onion powder, salt, and pepper.
2. Dip steaks in buttermilk, then dredge in the flour mixture.
3. Heat oil in a skillet over medium-high heat. Fry steaks for 3-4 minutes per side, until golden brown.
4. Drain on paper towels and serve with gravy.

Pralines

Ingredients:

- 1 cup brown sugar
- 1/2 cup heavy cream
- 1/4 cup butter
- 1 tsp vanilla extract
- 1 1/2 cups pecans

Instructions:

1. In a saucepan, combine brown sugar, heavy cream, and butter. Bring to a boil over medium heat.
2. Cook for 5-7 minutes, stirring constantly. Remove from heat and stir in vanilla extract and pecans.
3. Drop spoonfuls of the mixture onto parchment paper and let cool to set.

Brunswick Stew

Ingredients:

- 1 lb chicken, cooked and shredded
- 1 lb pork shoulder, cooked and shredded
- 1 can diced tomatoes (14.5 oz)
- 1 can corn kernels (15 oz)
- 1 can lima beans (15 oz)
- 1 onion, diced
- 2 cloves garlic, minced
- 1 tsp thyme
- 1 tsp paprika
- 4 cups chicken broth
- 2 tbsp Worcestershire sauce
- Salt and pepper to taste

Instructions:

1. In a large pot, combine shredded chicken, pork, tomatoes, corn, lima beans, onion, garlic, thyme, paprika, chicken broth, and Worcestershire sauce.
2. Bring to a boil, then reduce heat and simmer for 45 minutes, stirring occasionally.
3. Season with salt and pepper and serve.

Pimento Cheese

Ingredients:

- 2 cups sharp cheddar cheese, shredded
- 1 cup cream cheese, softened
- 1/2 cup mayonnaise
- 1/4 cup jarred pimentos, drained and chopped
- 1 tbsp Dijon mustard
- 1/2 tsp garlic powder
- Salt and pepper to taste

Instructions:

1. In a mixing bowl, combine shredded cheddar, cream cheese, mayonnaise, pimentos, Dijon mustard, and garlic powder.
2. Stir well until everything is evenly mixed.
3. Season with salt and pepper to taste.
4. Chill in the refrigerator for at least an hour before serving with crackers, bread, or as a sandwich spread.

Po' Boy Sandwiches

Ingredients:

- 4 hoagie rolls
- 1 lb shrimp, peeled and deveined
- 1 cup flour
- 1/2 cup cornmeal
- 1 tsp paprika
- 1/2 tsp cayenne pepper
- Salt and pepper to taste
- 2 cups vegetable oil for frying
- Lettuce, tomatoes, pickles for garnish
- Remoulade sauce or tartar sauce

Instructions:

1. In a shallow bowl, mix flour, cornmeal, paprika, cayenne, salt, and pepper.
2. Dredge shrimp in the flour mixture.
3. Heat oil in a skillet over medium heat. Fry shrimp in batches for 2-3 minutes per side until crispy.
4. Toast hoagie rolls and spread with remoulade or tartar sauce.
5. Assemble the po' boys with shrimp, lettuce, tomato, and pickles. Serve immediately.

Low Country Boil

Ingredients:

- 1 lb shrimp, peeled and deveined
- 1 lb sausage (such as Andouille), sliced
- 4 ears corn, cut into thirds
- 2 lbs baby potatoes
- 2 tbsp Old Bay seasoning
- 1 lemon, quartered
- 6 cloves garlic, smashed
- 8 cups water
- Salt to taste

Instructions:

1. In a large pot, bring water to a boil and add garlic, lemon, Old Bay seasoning, and salt.
2. Add potatoes and cook for 15 minutes.
3. Add sausage and corn, cook for another 10 minutes.
4. Add shrimp and cook for 3-5 minutes until shrimp are pink and cooked through.
5. Drain and pour everything out onto a platter. Serve with extra lemon wedges.

Oysters Rockefeller

Ingredients:

- 12 fresh oysters, shucked
- 2 tbsp butter
- 2 cloves garlic, minced
- 1/2 cup spinach, chopped
- 1/4 cup breadcrumbs
- 1/4 cup Parmesan cheese
- 1/4 cup Pernod or white wine
- 1/4 cup heavy cream
- Salt and pepper to taste

Instructions:

1. Preheat the oven to 400°F (200°C).
2. In a pan, melt butter and sauté garlic for 1 minute.
3. Add spinach and cook until wilted, about 2-3 minutes.
4. Stir in breadcrumbs, Parmesan, Pernod, and cream. Cook until mixture thickens.
5. Spoon the mixture onto each oyster and bake for 10-12 minutes until golden and bubbly.

Baked Macaroni and Cheese

Ingredients:

- 1 lb elbow macaroni, cooked
- 3 cups shredded sharp cheddar cheese
- 1 cup shredded mozzarella cheese
- 2 cups milk
- 1/4 cup butter
- 1/4 cup flour
- 1 tsp mustard powder
- 1/2 tsp paprika
- Salt and pepper to taste
- 1/2 cup breadcrumbs

Instructions:

1. Preheat oven to 350°F (175°C).
2. In a saucepan, melt butter over medium heat. Stir in flour, mustard powder, and paprika to make a roux.
3. Gradually whisk in milk, cooking until the sauce thickens, about 5-7 minutes.
4. Remove from heat and stir in cheese until melted.
5. Mix the cooked macaroni with the cheese sauce. Pour into a greased baking dish.

6. Top with breadcrumbs and bake for 25-30 minutes until golden and bubbly.

Fried Okra

Ingredients:

- 1 lb fresh okra, sliced into 1/2-inch rounds
- 1 cup cornmeal
- 1/2 cup flour
- 1 tsp paprika
- 1/2 tsp cayenne pepper
- Salt and pepper to taste
- Vegetable oil for frying

Instructions:

1. In a bowl, mix cornmeal, flour, paprika, cayenne, salt, and pepper.
2. Dredge okra slices in the cornmeal mixture.
3. Heat oil in a skillet over medium-high heat. Fry okra for 3-4 minutes until golden and crispy.
4. Drain on paper towels and serve hot.

Chicken and Dumplings

Ingredients:

- 2 chicken breasts, cooked and shredded
- 4 cups chicken broth
- 2 cups milk
- 1 onion, diced
- 2 carrots, diced
- 2 celery stalks, diced
- 2 cups flour
- 1 tbsp baking powder
- 1/2 tsp salt
- 1/4 tsp pepper
- 2 tbsp butter
- 1/2 cup milk (for dumplings)

Instructions:

1. In a large pot, bring chicken broth and milk to a simmer.
2. Add onion, carrots, and celery, and cook for 10-12 minutes.
3. In a bowl, combine flour, baking powder, salt, and pepper. Stir in butter and milk to form a dough for dumplings.
4. Drop spoonfuls of dough into the simmering broth and cook for 10-12 minutes.

5. Add shredded chicken and cook for another 5 minutes until heated through. Serve hot.

Sausage Gravy

Ingredients:

- 1 lb breakfast sausage
- 1/4 cup flour
- 2 cups milk
- Salt and pepper to taste

Instructions:

1. In a skillet, cook sausage over medium heat until browned.
2. Stir in flour and cook for 2-3 minutes to form a roux.
3. Gradually whisk in milk and cook until the gravy thickens, about 5-7 minutes.
4. Season with salt and pepper to taste. Serve over biscuits or toast.

Shrimp Creole

Ingredients:

- 1 lb shrimp, peeled and deveined
- 1 onion, diced
- 1 bell pepper, diced
- 2 cloves garlic, minced
- 1 can diced tomatoes (14.5 oz)
- 1/2 cup chicken broth
- 1 tsp paprika
- 1 tsp thyme
- 1/2 tsp cayenne pepper
- 1 tbsp parsley, chopped
- Cooked rice for serving

Instructions:

1. In a large skillet, sauté onion, bell pepper, and garlic until soft.
2. Add tomatoes, chicken broth, paprika, thyme, and cayenne. Simmer for 10 minutes.
3. Add shrimp and cook for 3-4 minutes until pink and cooked through.
4. Serve over cooked rice and garnish with parsley.

Peach Cobbler

Ingredients:

- 4 cups fresh or canned peaches, drained
- 1/2 cup sugar
- 1 tbsp lemon juice
- 1 tsp cinnamon
- 1/4 tsp nutmeg
- 1 cup flour
- 1 tsp baking powder
- 1/2 tsp salt
- 1/4 cup butter, melted
- 3/4 cup milk

Instructions:

1. Preheat oven to 350°F (175°C).
2. In a bowl, toss peaches with sugar, lemon juice, cinnamon, and nutmeg. Spread in a baking dish.
3. In another bowl, mix flour, baking powder, salt, melted butter, and milk. Pour over peaches.
4. Bake for 40-45 minutes until golden brown and bubbly. Serve warm with ice cream or whipped cream.

Beignets

Ingredients:

- 2 cups all-purpose flour
- 1/4 cup granulated sugar
- 1 tbsp active dry yeast
- 1/2 tsp salt
- 1/2 cup warm water
- 1/4 cup milk, warm
- 2 eggs, beaten
- 1/4 cup unsalted butter, melted
- Vegetable oil for frying
- Powdered sugar for dusting

Instructions:

1. In a large bowl, combine flour, sugar, yeast, and salt.
2. In a separate bowl, combine warm water, milk, eggs, and melted butter. Gradually add the wet mixture to the dry ingredients, stirring until the dough forms.
3. Knead the dough on a floured surface for about 5 minutes.
4. Cover the dough and let it rise in a warm place for 1-2 hours or until doubled in size.
5. Heat oil in a large pot to 375°F (190°C).

6. Roll out the dough to about 1/4-inch thickness and cut into squares.

7. Fry the dough pieces in batches for 2-3 minutes, turning occasionally, until golden brown.

8. Drain on paper towels and dust with powdered sugar. Serve hot.

Bourbon Street Steak

Ingredients:

- 2 boneless ribeye steaks
- 1/4 cup bourbon
- 2 tbsp soy sauce
- 2 tbsp olive oil
- 2 cloves garlic, minced
- 1 tbsp Worcestershire sauce
- 1 tsp Dijon mustard
- Salt and pepper to taste

Instructions:

1. In a small bowl, whisk together bourbon, soy sauce, olive oil, garlic, Worcestershire sauce, mustard, salt, and pepper.
2. Pour the marinade over the steaks and refrigerate for at least 1 hour.
3. Preheat a grill or skillet over medium-high heat.
4. Grill the steaks for 4-6 minutes per side, or until the desired doneness is reached.
5. Let the steaks rest for a few minutes before serving.

Muffuletta Sandwich

Ingredients:

- 1 large round loaf of Italian bread
- 1/2 lb sliced salami
- 1/2 lb sliced ham
- 1/2 lb sliced mortadella
- 1/2 lb sliced provolone cheese
- 1/2 cup olive salad (purchased or homemade)

Instructions:

1. Slice the bread in half horizontally.
2. Layer the meats and cheese on the bottom half of the bread.
3. Spoon the olive salad over the top and spread evenly.
4. Place the top of the bread on and press down gently.
5. Wrap the sandwich in plastic wrap and refrigerate for at least 1 hour to allow the flavors to meld.
6. Slice and serve.

Southern-style Deviled Eggs

Ingredients:

- 6 large eggs, hard-boiled and peeled
- 1/4 cup mayonnaise
- 1 tbsp Dijon mustard
- 1 tsp white vinegar
- 1/4 tsp paprika
- Salt and pepper to taste
- Chopped chives for garnish

Instructions:

1. Cut the boiled eggs in half lengthwise and remove the yolks.
2. Mash the yolks in a bowl and mix with mayonnaise, mustard, vinegar, paprika, salt, and pepper.
3. Spoon or pipe the yolk mixture back into the egg whites.
4. Garnish with chopped chives and a sprinkle of paprika.
5. Serve chilled.

Southern Corn Pudding

Ingredients:

- 2 cans (15 oz each) creamed corn
- 1 cup whole kernel corn, drained
- 1/2 cup heavy cream
- 2 eggs, beaten
- 1/4 cup sugar
- 1/4 cup unsalted butter, melted
- 1 tsp vanilla extract
- 1/2 tsp salt
- 1/2 tsp ground black pepper

Instructions:

1. Preheat the oven to 350°F (175°C).
2. In a large bowl, combine creamed corn, whole kernel corn, heavy cream, eggs, sugar, butter, vanilla, salt, and pepper.
3. Pour the mixture into a greased baking dish.
4. Bake for 45-50 minutes, or until golden brown and set.
5. Let cool slightly before serving.

Collard Greens and Ham Hocks

Ingredients:

- 2 bunches collard greens, washed and chopped
- 2 ham hocks
- 1 onion, chopped
- 4 cloves garlic, minced
- 4 cups chicken broth
- 1 tsp salt
- 1/2 tsp black pepper
- 1 tsp crushed red pepper flakes (optional)
- 1 tbsp vinegar

Instructions:

1. In a large pot, combine collard greens, ham hocks, onion, garlic, and chicken broth.
2. Bring to a boil, then reduce the heat and simmer for 1.5-2 hours, or until the greens are tender.
3. Remove the ham hocks, shred the meat, and return it to the pot.
4. Stir in vinegar and season with salt, pepper, and red pepper flakes.
5. Serve hot.

Pecan-Crusted Chicken

Ingredients:

- 4 boneless, skinless chicken breasts
- 1 cup pecans, chopped
- 1/2 cup breadcrumbs
- 1 egg, beaten
- 1/4 cup Dijon mustard
- Salt and pepper to taste
- 2 tbsp olive oil

Instructions:

1. Preheat the oven to 375°F (190°C).
2. In a shallow bowl, mix the pecans, breadcrumbs, salt, and pepper.
3. Brush the chicken breasts with Dijon mustard and dip them into the pecan mixture, pressing down to coat evenly.
4. Heat olive oil in a skillet over medium-high heat.
5. Brown the chicken breasts on both sides (about 2-3 minutes per side).
6. Transfer the chicken to a baking dish and bake for 20-25 minutes, or until fully cooked.

Chicken and Sausage Gumbo

Ingredients:

- 2 chicken breasts, cubed
- 1 lb Andouille sausage, sliced
- 1 onion, chopped
- 1 bell pepper, chopped
- 2 celery stalks, chopped
- 4 cloves garlic, minced
- 6 cups chicken broth
- 1 can (14.5 oz) diced tomatoes
- 1 tsp thyme
- 1 tsp smoked paprika
- 1/2 tsp cayenne pepper
- 1/4 cup flour
- 1/4 cup vegetable oil
- Salt and pepper to taste
- Cooked rice for serving

Instructions:

1. In a large pot, heat the oil over medium heat. Stir in the flour to make a roux and cook for about 5-7 minutes until dark brown.

2. Add the onions, bell pepper, celery, and garlic to the roux. Cook until softened, about 5 minutes.

3. Add chicken, sausage, broth, tomatoes, thyme, paprika, and cayenne. Bring to a boil.

4. Reduce the heat and simmer for 45 minutes.

5. Serve over cooked rice.

Country Ham

Ingredients:

- 1 cured country ham (about 5-7 lbs)
- 2 cups water
- 1/2 cup brown sugar
- 1/4 cup Dijon mustard

Instructions:

1. Preheat the oven to 325°F (165°C).
2. Place the ham in a roasting pan and pour water around it.
3. Cover with aluminum foil and bake for 2.5-3 hours, basting occasionally.
4. Mix the brown sugar and mustard to make a glaze.
5. During the last 30 minutes of baking, brush the ham with the glaze and continue to bake uncovered until caramelized.
6. Slice and serve.

Boiled Peanuts

Ingredients:

- 1 lb raw peanuts (in the shell)
- 4 cups water
- 1/4 cup salt
- 1 tbsp Cajun seasoning (optional)

Instructions:

1. Place the peanuts in a large pot and cover with water.
2. Add salt and Cajun seasoning (if using).
3. Bring to a boil, then reduce the heat and simmer for 2-3 hours, or until the peanuts are tender.
4. Drain and serve warm.

Sweet Tea

Ingredients:

- 4-6 black tea bags
- 1 cup sugar
- 4 cups water
- Ice
- Lemon slices (optional)

Instructions:

1. Bring 4 cups of water to a boil in a saucepan.
2. Add the tea bags and steep for 5-7 minutes.
3. Remove the tea bags and stir in the sugar until dissolved.
4. Pour the tea into a large pitcher and add 4 cups of cold water.
5. Let it cool to room temperature, then refrigerate until chilled.
6. Serve over ice and garnish with lemon slices, if desired.

Fish Fry

Ingredients:

- 4 fish fillets (catfish, tilapia, or your choice)
- 1 cup cornmeal
- 1/2 cup flour
- 1 tsp paprika
- 1 tsp garlic powder
- 1 tsp salt
- 1/2 tsp black pepper
- 1/4 tsp cayenne pepper (optional)
- Vegetable oil for frying
- Lemon wedges (for serving)

Instructions:

1. In a shallow bowl, combine cornmeal, flour, paprika, garlic powder, salt, pepper, and cayenne.
2. Dredge the fish fillets in the cornmeal mixture, coating evenly.
3. Heat oil in a large skillet over medium-high heat.
4. Fry the fish fillets for 3-4 minutes per side, or until golden and crispy.
5. Drain on paper towels and serve with lemon wedges.

Chitlins (Chitterlings)

Ingredients:

- 5 lbs chitterlings, cleaned
- 1 onion, chopped
- 2 cloves garlic, minced
- 2 tbsp vinegar
- 1 tbsp salt
- 1/2 tsp black pepper
- 1/4 tsp cayenne pepper
- 4 cups water
- 2 tbsp vegetable oil

Instructions:

1. Rinse and clean the chitterlings thoroughly.
2. In a large pot, heat oil over medium heat and sauté the onion and garlic until softened.
3. Add the chitterlings, water, vinegar, salt, pepper, and cayenne.
4. Bring to a boil, then reduce to a simmer and cook for 2-3 hours until tender.
5. Drain, season with additional salt and pepper if needed, and serve.

Grits Casserole

Ingredients:

- 2 cups cooked grits (coarse or quick-cooking)
- 1/2 cup milk
- 1/2 cup shredded cheddar cheese
- 1/4 cup grated Parmesan cheese
- 1/2 cup butter, melted
- 2 eggs, beaten
- 1/2 tsp garlic powder
- Salt and pepper to taste

Instructions:

1. Preheat the oven to 350°F (175°C).
2. In a large bowl, combine cooked grits, milk, cheddar cheese, Parmesan cheese, butter, eggs, garlic powder, salt, and pepper.
3. Pour the mixture into a greased casserole dish and bake for 30-35 minutes, or until set and lightly browned on top.
4. Let it cool for a few minutes before serving.

Fried Catfish

Ingredients:

- 4 catfish fillets
- 1 cup cornmeal
- 1/2 cup flour
- 1 tsp paprika
- 1 tsp garlic powder
- 1/2 tsp salt
- 1/2 tsp black pepper
- Vegetable oil for frying
- Lemon wedges (for serving)

Instructions:

1. In a shallow dish, combine cornmeal, flour, paprika, garlic powder, salt, and pepper.
2. Dredge the catfish fillets in the cornmeal mixture, pressing down gently to coat.
3. Heat oil in a large skillet over medium-high heat.
4. Fry the catfish for 4-5 minutes per side, or until golden brown and crispy.
5. Drain on paper towels and serve with lemon wedges.

Chicken-Liver Pâté

Ingredients:

- 1 lb chicken livers, cleaned
- 1/2 onion, chopped
- 2 cloves garlic, minced
- 1/4 cup brandy or cognac
- 1/2 cup heavy cream
- 1/4 cup butter
- 1/2 tsp thyme
- Salt and pepper to taste

Instructions:

1. In a skillet, melt butter over medium heat and sauté the onions and garlic until softened.
2. Add the chicken livers and cook for 5-7 minutes, until browned and cooked through.
3. Pour in the brandy and cook for another 2 minutes.
4. Transfer the liver mixture to a food processor and blend with heavy cream, thyme, salt, and pepper until smooth.
5. Chill in the refrigerator for at least 2 hours before serving with crackers or toast.

Baked Beans with Bacon

Ingredients:

- 2 cans (15 oz each) baked beans
- 4 slices bacon, chopped
- 1/2 onion, chopped
- 1/4 cup brown sugar
- 1 tbsp Dijon mustard
- 1 tbsp Worcestershire sauce
- 1/4 tsp black pepper

Instructions:

1. Preheat the oven to 350°F (175°C).
2. In a skillet, cook the bacon over medium heat until crispy.
3. Remove the bacon and sauté the onion in the bacon fat until softened.
4. In a baking dish, combine the baked beans, cooked bacon, sautéed onion, brown sugar, mustard, Worcestershire sauce, and black pepper.
5. Bake for 30-40 minutes, stirring occasionally, until bubbly and caramelized.

Mississippi Mud Pie

Ingredients:

- 1 pre-baked chocolate pie crust
- 1 cup heavy cream
- 1/2 cup butter, softened
- 1/2 cup brown sugar
- 1/4 cup cocoa powder
- 2 large eggs
- 1 tsp vanilla extract
- 1/4 tsp salt
- 1 cup mini marshmallows
- 1/2 cup crushed graham crackers (for topping)

Instructions:

1. Preheat the oven to 350°F (175°C).
2. In a saucepan, melt butter over medium heat, then stir in the brown sugar and cocoa powder.
3. Add the eggs, one at a time, whisking after each addition. Stir in vanilla and salt.
4. Pour the mixture into the pre-baked chocolate pie crust.
5. Bake for 25-30 minutes, or until set.
6. In the last 5 minutes of baking, add marshmallows to the top of the pie.

7. Let the pie cool completely, then top with crushed graham crackers before serving.

www.ingramcontent.com/pod-product-compliance
Lightning Source LLC
LaVergne TN
LVHW081319060526
838201LV00055B/2362